Lead like the Best

A Strategic Guide to Leadership & Organizational Success

ALFORD SIMON

PUBLISHING

Lead like the Best: *A Strategic Guide to Leadership & Organizational Success*
Copyright © 2017 by Alford Simon

Published by:
Divine Desires Publishing
P.O. Box 33200
Fort Worth, TX 76132
www.divinedesires.org

Printed in the United States of America

Divine Desires Publishing, 2017

ISBN-13: 978-0998251202 (Divine Desires)
ISBN-10: 0998251208

PUBLISHING

PRAISE FOR LEAD LIKE THE BEST

"I have read "Lead like the Best" and must say that I was impressed with the basics this book covered. Alford has done a good job defining leadership principles as well as providing the reader with anecdotal examples that makes the book relatable and understandable to the reader. For the new leader, this book offers help in developing leadership skills and for those who are mature in leadership, the book serves as a reminder of some of the principles that may have been forgotten."

~LaSharnda Beckwith, PhD.
Dean, College of Business & Management, (HIU)

"Leadership is your responsibility. Whatever capacity that you serve as a leader, Lead like the Best will assist you in becoming your best both personally and professionally. This book will give you the necessary tools to become an effective leader. Lead like the Best, will help you become the person of influence you were born to be."

~Dr. Regina Spellmon
Pastor of Ambassadors Today

"Lead like the BEST is an insightful and practical guide that gives us a candid look at the journey of leadership. We find comfort because Master Life Coach, Alford Simon lends his climbing expertise and does not allow the reader to journey alone, he takes the journey with you. Lead like the BEST is liberating. We get permission to face what we always thought was impossible while learning new strategies, discovering new resources and finding renewed strength that turns the impossible into possible. It is a must read for those who are looking for a guide to not just help them be a good leader, this book is for those who desire to Lead like the BEST! Let the journey begin!"

~Dr. Connie Stewart, Master Life Coach
Life in Bloom Life Coach Institute & Bloom University

CONTENTS

Introduction -------------------------**Page 9**

Chapter 1 --------------------------**Page 17**
Personal Development

Chapter 2 --------------------------**Page 35**
Self-Discipline

Chapter 3 --------------------------**Page 51**
The Mission

Chapter 4 --------------------------**Page 65**
Possessing an Effective Team

Chapter 5 --------------------------**Page 81**
Developing The Team

Chapter 6 --------------------------**Page 97**
Casting The Vision

Chapter 7 --------------------------**Page 113**
Servant Leadership

To my God,

Because of your commission to me to write this book I was able to complete it in 30 days. I thank you for your spiritual wisdom, insight, and understanding on how to go about finishing this project. Your supernatural strength led me through when I was weak and tired. Your right hand held me up when I wanted to give in. Thank you because without you my life would not be possible.

To my Wife,

I am thankful and grateful to God for the encouragement and motivation that you give me. You are my biggest inspiration and the greatest help mate that I could ever ask for. You were my strength and my rock even when I doubted myself. Without your wisdom, knowledge, and guidance this book would not have been possible. I love you and thank you.

To my Family,

Your support throughout this process has been invaluable. You all helped me by giving me your assistance and honest opinion when I needed it the most. This book was created by the long phone calls and meetings we constantly had concerning this masterpiece. I love and thank you all for your support and constant encouragement.

To my Followers,
    Without you this book would truly not have been possible.
You are literally the reason God commissioned me to write this
book. Your questions and concerns led to many of the topics this
book covers and the questions it answers. I thank you for your
constant support and love.

To my Peers, Colleagues, and Teachers,
    I thank you for your continued support and push through-
out the process of writing this book. Because of the knowledge
that you all poured into me I was able to complete this book. I
thank God for you'll and appreciate all that you all have done for
me.

To my Readers,
    I hope and pray this book answers many of the questions
you have and assists you as you climb the mountain of leadership. This journey can be difficult and lonely at times, but I
believe that this book is an extension of me. You are not alone in
this journey and I hope the guidance I offer in this book helps you
to achieve success while leading like the best!

"Everyone wants to be a
Leader
But are you ready
take the **CLIMB?**"

INTRODUCTION

Here you are, faced with a mountain. This mountain is higher than Mt. Everest and bigger than any challenge you have ever taken on before. Many have endeavored to climb this mountain before you and failed, while others have even died in the process of trying to scale such a large structure. Yet you are faced with this mountain and it still calls out to you. Knowing that failure is possible and death is near, you still face the mountain of impossibilities, and instead of seeing and hearing the word impossible, you hear the phrase "I'm-Possible" instead.

At this mountain you ponder the thought, can I climb like the **BEST**? Can I really achieve what the **BEST** have achieved? Can I scale this mountain of impossibilities and make it possible like the best have done before me? This mountain is scary not because of how it looks; because the view is beautiful. This mountain is scary because of the journey that you will have to endure to make it to the summit and to attain your goal of success.

And as you stare at the mountain with anticipation and fear, you hear the cries of men falling on their journey up the mountain. But you also hear the joyous bellow triumph of men that have achieved the impossible. The name of this mountain is Leadership. And it is the most dangerous yet most fulfilling journey you will ever take. Are you ready to climb? Are you ready to **Lead like the BEST**? If so, let's take a journey up this mountain of impossibilities together.

Leadership is a mountain that many men endeavor to climb, yet fail in the process of pursuit. They have the tenacity to take the journey, yet don't possess the stamina or determination in many cases to finish what they have started. I was inspired to write this book to help you understand the journey of leadership because I know what it's like to have a gift without a guide. I understand what it feels like to want to be the **BEST**, but still yet lack the **BEST** resources to help me do so. For this reason, I know leadership is not something that should be embarked upon without the right mentality and without the right tools. Therefore, I put together the **BEST** tools to help you achieve the **BEST** results.

WHAT IS LEADERSHIP

Before we can take a journey a few questions must first be answered such as what is leadership? The leader-

INTRODUCTION

ship Guru John Maxwell defines leadership as "influence" and influence is defined as "the capacity to have an effect on the character, development, or behavior of someone or something." We can see that leadership therefore means the amount of effect a person has on another individual's character, development, or behavior. Leadership, in layman terms, is the ability to impact someone's life positively or negatively.

So stop and think. Whose life (character, development, behavior, attitude, etc.) are you impacting and are you impacting it positively? The best leaders impact their followers' lives positively in a multitude of ways, and leave a lasting impression that cannot be ignored.

Leadership to me is influence also, but is also about the journey and how you use that power (influence) to steer the course of your own life and the lives of others. Having a leadership position means to possess power over those that are under you, but if the power you hold is abused, are you a leader or a tyrant? Leaders are for the people; tyrants are for themselves. So in essence, leadership is about service and sacrifice and if you are not serving and sacrificing for those who follow you then the title of leader may not suit you. Remember, if service is beneath you, leadership is beyond you.

No great leader has ever become great without serving first. Serving your way to influence and gaining peoples trust is a better leadership model than flaunting your authority around and making people submit to you out of fear. Connection over position should always be the way that leadership is built in any group or organization, because as one of my favorite speakers and mentors Jonathan Sprinkles says, "Connection is Key". Where there is no connection, there will be no key to unlock the door to success in any organization, group, career, or endeavor. Good, connected, service oriented leadership is the path one should follow to achieve success, because that is what leadership is all about.

WHO CAN BE A LEADER

Another question we have to answer before starting the journey is, who can be a leader? I believe to answer this question a myth must first be debunked and that myth is "Leaders are born". Many people blame faith, God, or some outside spiritual force for the creation of great leaders. Although I believe that may have its place, it is not the entire reason for great leadership. Leaders are not born, they are made. I have met many great men and women with almost supernatural leadership abilities, but because they are selfish, arrogant, and prideful, they will never become great leaders and will always be good managers.

Leadership many times is more about who you are more so than what you have. You can possess almost no talent in any area and still be a good leader because of how you treat people. People are influenced by who you are not what you have and when whom you are shines bright, that light draws people to you. If you continue to "Let it Shine" as the old hymn states being a leader will be a possibility for you. Anyone with a light that can draw people and influence them can be a leader.

Leaders can be found in every area of society. Almost everyone in the world is a leader in some way, form, or fashion because they are impacting someone's life. This should make you feel better because this lets you know that you are a leader but it's not about just being a leader, it's about being the **BEST** leader. Leaders come a dime a dozen but the **BEST** leaders are a rare phenomenon to find. So to answer the question; anyone can be a leader, and almost everyone is a leader, but the true question is, are you willing to be one of the **BEST** leaders?

WHY TAKE THE JOURNEY

The last question we must answer is why take such a dangerous journey? Why embark on the journey of not only being a leader but becoming one of the **BEST** leaders? Well that is a question you will have to look deep inside to answer.

You are at a mountain and as you stand at the base of this impossible mountain, you are presented with two options. Do I climb and try to become the **BEST** there ever was or do I shy away into obscurity and live a life filled with "What-if's"? What if I had taken a chance? What if I had the courage? What if I lost everything? What if I gained the world? At this mountain you realize life is full of **"What-if's"**, and one is standing tall and intimidating right before you. Will you climb, will you take a chance, will you sacrifice everything to be the **BEST?**

THE CHOICE IS YOURS!

Remember you need the best tools to achieve the best results. If you have decided to embark upon this journey, then read this book if you dare and use the tools in it so that you can achieve success.

Alford Simon

"Every person that has

Plan to Grow

must have a

Budget to Grow

because if you don't invest in yourself

no one will invest in you"

CHAPTER 1

Personal Development

The Story of an NBA Superstar

An NBA superstar was born in New York on February 17, 1963. He was the fourth of five children born to James and Deloris. James was a mechanic, and Deloris was a bank teller. Soon after his birth, James and Deloris felt that the streets of Brooklyn were unsafe to raise a family, so they moved the family to Wilmington, North Carolina.

As a young man, this soon to be superstar, immediately became interested in sports. Baseball would be his first love, but would not be the sport he became successful in. He would play catch in the yard with his father, who loved baseball, but soon started to play basketball to try and follow in the footsteps of his older brother, whom he idolized growing up.

At Laney High School, when he was a sophomore, he decided to try out for the varsity basketball team. But in his pursuit to achieve this endeavor he was prematurely cut due to his short stature, lanky body, and his lack of overall ability at basketball (he basically sucked). The following summer, he grew four inches, and practiced tirelessly every day. He worked hard and didn't give up on his dream to be successful in the sport he was trying to pursue.

> **PAUSE:** What dreams, goals, and aspirations have you given up on because people, circumstances, or YOU decided that you weren't good enough?

_____

_____

_____

_____

_____

_____

_____

His hard work, dedication, and commitment paid off when he averaged 25 points per game in his last two years of high school and was selected to be on the "McDonald's All-American Team" as a senior.

After his high school tenure, he received a basketball scholarship from the University of North Carolina where he would play under the famous college coach Dean Smith. In his first year of college basketball, he was named the ACC Freshman of the Year. He would help lead UNC to the 1982 NCAA Championship, and would make the game-winning shot.

After winning the Naismith College Player of the Year award in 1984, He would then leave North Carolina to enter the NBA draft. Although he decided to leave college early, he later returned to the University in 1986 to complete his degree in geography.

In the 1984 NBA draft, he was selected as the third overall draft pick and was picked up by the Chicago Bulls. As a rookie on the team, he made an immediate impact by averaging 28.2 points a game, including six where he would score 40+ points. He was selected to participate in the NBA All-Star Game and was named Rookie of the Year. This would be just the beginning of a career filled with awards and accolades. During the following years of his career, he would go on to achieve five regular season MVP awards, three All-Star game MVP awards, six NBA Finals MVP awards, six NBA championships, and a defensive player of the year award. The name of this legendary athlete was Michael Jordan.

The Importance of Personal Development

Michael was able to achieve what he did, not because he was born with raw talent or because he had a gift; but because he possessed great work ethic and understood the importance of practice. Many times in life we want things easy, and we don't like to practice for them. We want easy money, fame, jobs, women & men, weight loss, and overall easy lives. But there is an old saying "EASY COME, EASY GO"; which means, if everything comes easy the easier it will be for us to lose them also.

Personal Development is not only important, but critical when you are trying to achieve more in life than the average person. Most people never push themselves to their full capacity and therefore never obtain all they were meant to possess in life.

THE FORMULA

At one point in my past I wanted things to be easy, and because of that I never put in 100%. I gave 50% on my job, 50% in school, 50% in relationships, and 50% in life; and in the end, I was left only gaining about 25% of what I actually put in. This phenomenon baffled me because I was doing enough to get by, yet I wasn't receiving back what I put in. Then it hit me! If I give 50%, then my return on that will only be half of what I actually put in.

Let me give you an example: If I put in 50% on homework and gain back only 25%, I will make a 75% on my paper. Why? Because I already put in 50% which is my base and my return will be 25% (50%+25%=75%). Therefore, if I consistently put only 50% in life, I would never receive a full return on what I placed in, and the result would be that I would never reach my full capacity or capabilities.

Then I changed my mindset. I understood to live a decent life with a full return I would need to put in at least 67% which would give me a 33% return and therefore would put me at a full return of 100% in life (67%+33%=100%). But I didn't just want to live decently, I wanted to thrive. I wanted to be successful. I wanted to have a mansion, not just a house, and a Bentley not just a Honda. So I understood that in order to receive not just a return but an increase, I would have to live life above 67% so that I would have an overflow of abundance in my lifestyle.

Personal Development, for this reason, becomes not just important but critical. Without studying, learning, or growing, most people can get by in life, put in 50% and receive that 75% return. But they will always live paycheck to paycheck and will always just get by. They will never have enough to save, travel, give, retire, or live a good life. They will stay worried, stressed out, and overwhelmed because they choose to live life with talents, but never turn those talents into substance.

To live a life that is above 50% one must begin the process of actually putting to work and learning the importance of personal development. Personal development involves activities that improve awareness and identity, develops talents and potential, builds human capital while facilitating employability, enhances the quality of life, and contributes to the realization of dreams and aspirations. In simple terms, personal development is the process by which an individual becomes better and increases in capacity. Personal development can be used to help individuals in many different areas that they deem necessary and critical.

Personal development is critical to leaders in that it keeps the leader learning, growing, and prospering in their specified fields. If leaders do not embrace personal development as a priority, they are putting themselves and their organizations in a detrimental position. Personal Development is one of the keys to organizational success and if a leader is not committed to the process neither will those they lead. Personal development must be a lifestyle, not a fly by night commitment. Personal development is the backbone of every leader, and is the foundation from which they lead. The foundation of a leader must be firm and cannot be faulty, or else the house (organization) they build upon it will fall. Let's look at what leaders, and people in general can do to be successful in the area of personal development.

Books

There is a quote by Gilbert K. Chesterton which states:

"There is a great deal of difference between an eager man who wants to read a book and the tired man who wants a book to read."

–Gilbert K. Chesterton

This quote has always stuck out to me because it paints a picture of the lives of two very different individuals and how reading impacted their lives. The first picture shows someone who is energetic, ready to learn, and ready to succeed. It is the picture of an individual who didn't wait until life got bad to read, they did so beforehand, and therefore avoided many troubles. The second picture portrays an individual whose life has worn on them and made them tired. This individual now wants a book to read so that they can hopefully find an answer for what is occurring in their life.

> **PAUSE:** Which individual are you at this point in your life? What books are you reading and what books should you be reading?

_____
_____
_____
_____
_____
_____
_____

The moral of this quote is that, reading will find you somewhere in life but the real questions are "Where will it find you?" & "How will it find you?"

If personal development is a priority, reading also has to be. Books hold within their confines the ability to change your life, and the opportunity to enhance it. Books can answer many of the questions people have, while also assisting them in the process of solving many of their problems. Books are your link to the past, your connection to the present, and your access to the future.

Many times we as leaders have high hopes to connect with someone famous like John Maxwell, Steve Harvey, Les Brown, or other high profile speakers, leaders, and teachers that can mentor us. These mentors would be an awesome asset, but let's be honest it is almost impossible to connect with them personally unless you have a connection or money to pay for their time. Many of us don't have that type of priceless connection or that type of money, ($$$$) so we have to do the next best thing which is buying their book.

Books are your connection to high-profile mentors that you may never have the opportunity to connect with on a personal level. But although you can't pick their mind in person, you can always do so through the content inside of the many books, workbooks, manuals, and other written material they have produced. Many times you can learn $1,000,000 secrets from a $20 book, that can elevate your life and money into the million-dollar sphere if you put what you have learned into practice.

Mentors

Another great asset to leaders and individuals looking to grow in the area of personal development are mentors. Mentors are leaders that can POUR wisdom, knowledge, and understanding into you, concerning the areas in which you are trying to advance and develop in. They help give you the inside scoop on new developments in your field which keeps you ahead of the game, ahead of the market, and ahead of your competition. Mentors are a source of knowledge many people never tap into, because they don't have the tenacity to reach them.

Mentors do something I like to call **P.O.U.R** into you.

They Position, Open, Unite, and Refine you.

Let's break these words down:

Mentors **Position** you because they point you in the right direction with their wisdom and knowledge. They also position you for success by affording you the opportunity to know where they failed and where they succeeded

They **Open** you by awakening your mind to new possibilities that you may not have seen before. Their experience enables them to share opportunities, knowledge, and processes with you that you may not have encountered otherwise.

They **Unite** you with resources, tools, and influencers that can help you achieve your destiny and goals with less hassle.

And lastly, they **Refine** you. They correct, rebuke, and destroy old habits, mindset's, and processes you previously utilized that are either wrong or unreliable.

PAUSE: Do you have any mentors? Who? Do you see a need for mentors? What mentors are you/will you pursue?

_____
_____
_____
_____
_____
_____
_____

Mentors help us to see our lives, businesses, and leadership structures in a new light that affords us the opportunity to recreate greatness and not mediocrity. Many people live mediocre lives because they never listen to the wisdom of those who have walked out the process before them. Living life without guidance will always set us up for failure, while also placing us in detrimental situations and circumstances that could have been avoided if we listened to mentors.

Events

Going to different events and networking is also another way to commit to the process of personal development. A very influential mentor in my life always says,

You grow by the the places you go, the books you read, and the people you meet

-Dr. Regina Spellmon

I have found this saying to be true and have implemented it into my life. It has now become one of the key phrases I live by and teach those that I POUR into. The places you go assist in the process of personal development by placing you in the midst of connections that you would not have had otherwise. These connections might be the breakthrough you need to achieve your next level, or they may have a connect to the person you need to be connected to. Remember you are only 3-4 connections away from your dreams. Which means that though they may not be the missing link to your success, they might know someone who is.

Leaders and those trying to enhance themselves personally must also be intentional about attending different seminars and events that will afford them the opportunity to obtain more knowledge in their respective fields. Seminars and other educational settings help leaders to stay up to date on the nuances that may have occurred in their sector. It also helps those you lead to see your commitment to them, the organization, and yourself.

My personal experience with events has changed my life drastically for the better. I have attended many business seminars and workshops that have impacted my life and changed my perspective. These seminars and workshops were able to answer questions that I had been asking for years, and some I didn't even know I had. It was just what I needed to catapult my business and my life to new heights, while also take my speaking and leadership training skills to deeper depths of knowledge and insight. One of the events I attended even played a major part in me writing this book. Events have impacted my life, and that is why I now set aside money in my budget for events yearly. This money comes from my personal assets and is strictly for my personal development.

Every person that has a plan to grow must have a budget to grow because if you don't invest in yourself, no one will ever invest in you.

-Alford Simon

- - - - - - - - - - - - - - - -

PAUSE: What programs have you invested in? What is your budget for personal development? What programs do you plan on investing in?

_____

_____

_____

_____

_____

_____

Commitment to Values

In the process of personal development you must create, establish, and maintain a core set of values. Every leader needs a core set of values that they reference in times of uncertainty and in the middle of tough decisions. These values are the driving force behind a leader's motives and intentions when it comes to leading those who are under their charge. Many leaders never create this set of values, and therefore falter in the face of adversity. They give in to the pressures of being dishonest and unreliable, which makes them fall into the many traps that are set up for leaders.

One such example is that of President Bill Clinton. The Lewinsky scandal that plagued Clinton's career was a political sex scandal that came to light in 1998. It references a sexual relationship that occurred between 1995 and 1996 with the then 49-year-old President Bill Clinton and 22-year-old White House intern, Monica Lewinsky. During a speech on television, Clinton stated that he did not have sexual relations with Lewinsky. Through further investigation, it eventually led to charges of perjury and the impeachment of President Clinton in 1998 by the United States House of Representatives. It also led to his subsequent acquittal on all impeachment charges of perjury and obstruction of justice in a 21-day Senate trial. President Clinton was held in contempt of court by Judge Susan Webber Wright for providing a misleading testimony in the Paula Jones case regarding Monica Lewinsky and was fined $90,000. His license to practice law was suspended in

PERSONAL DEVELOPMENT

Arkansas for five years, and later by the United States Supreme Court.

All of this occurred because Clinton didn't have a clear set of values to fall back on in times of distress, temptation, and uncertainty. Having these values in place not only could have stopped the affair, but could have also avoided embarrassment for the entire country. If the leader of the free world can fall into temptation and lose his way, what makes us so different? We have to establish these values so that we will not fall into these destructive tendencies that seem to attack leadership. Leaders are the face of the people and the backbone of institutions; when they fall, so do those they lead. Possessing core values assist in blocking these attacks and stop these types of embarrassments for yourself and those you lead.

Core values position leaders for success so when obstacles come, they will be able to hurdle them with ease. When you have a clear set of values that you are committed to living your life by, no one or **"No-Thing"** can break through that commitment.

You may be wondering what these values look like. Well to many people they can be viewed from various perspectives. Some people's values come from their deep religious convictions, some come from morals their parents or family has instilled in them from youth, and many come from experience, or the culture they were raised in. All of these various life scenarios go into developing an effective set of core values that one can live their life by.

Examples of Core Values: Integrity, Honesty, Discipline, Commitment, and Positivity

> **PAUSE:** What are your core values? What core values do you plan on adding to your life?

_____

_____

_____

_____

_____

_____

_____

PERSONAL DEVELOPMENT

Many people are
WAITING
for someone to help them

Change

but change must first start with

Y.O.U

CHAPTER 2

Self-Discipline

Next, let's have a conversation about **"DISCIPLINE"** specifically self-discipline and its importance to leaders. Those in positions of authority have a necessity of being disciplined within themselves. Discipline is one of the major core values of leadership; and when it comes to first leading one's self, secondly leading organizations, and lastly leading people, it is especially needed.

Self-discipline is the practice of training one's self to obey certain rules, values, regulations, and restrictions that they have set for themselves. Another definition that is commonly used is self-control or the act of controlling one's self when presented with temptations or volatile situations. Leaders have to possess self-discipline, because if a leader cannot lead themselves, they will not be able to lead others.

Self-control is a necessity for leaders in both organizational and personal settings because it sets the tone of discipline for the rest of the body (those they lead). There is an old saying "what falls on the head will eventually flow to the body". This means that if the head (leader) of the organization does not have discipline in their actions, words, or work neither will those they lead. The spirit of the leader is what guides the spirit of the organization and those that work in it. If the leader's spirit is not in alignment, those that they lead will be out of alignment. The leader has to possess a mentality of excellence and a spirit of discipline for the organization to possess these same traits.

> **PAUSE:** Do you think self-discipline/self-control is a necessity when leading others? What experiences have you had with self-control; good or bad?

_____

_____

_____

_____

_____

_____

_____

P.U.S.H

Those that truly embody the element of self-discipline are athletes. Professional athletes, especially Olympians, have a special tolerance for pain and possess a unique endurance level. They train day in and day out to attain the level of success they want in their particular sports. They **PUSH** through their pain, their emotions, their fears, and their anxieties to achieve their desired outcome from their bodies so that they can win the gold medal they have worked so hard for.

They have a special **PUSH** in them that makes them keep on going even when things get hard. I believe they have this **PUSH** because they understand what the definition of **PUSH** is: *Persist, Until, Something, Happens* **(P.U.S.H).** Athletes not only understand this definition, but they have put it to work in their daily lives and careers.

Let's Break this **P.U.S.H** acronym down:

PERSIST:

To persist means to keep pushing in the face of adversity; to not give up or give in just because situations and circumstances are not lining up the way that you want them to. Everything is not going to go exactly the way you planned it; but just because it doesn't, that does not mean it's time for you to throw in the towel. Leaders must stay persistent and consistent so that they will see the fruits of their labor. They cannot give up when the going gets rough.

UNTIL:

Until is a place in time that involves waiting. Many people give up at this phase because they don't like the process that is involved. People want the promise, but never want to endure the process in order to achieve it. Their lives revolve around their now (present) circumstances and situations, so they never give thought to planning and preparing for their latter (future). Leaders must endure the process so they can be prepared for the promise.

SOMETHING:

Something represents the small breaks that happen on one's journey due to waiting and persistency. Something might not be the THING, or the big break, but it is Some-Thing, or small incremental increases that aid in the process of the big break.

HAPPENS:

Happens is the big break that everyone dreams about. It is the place where your persistence, waiting, and small breaks push you into the place of thriving and prospering you have been hoping for. This is where your business, life, or organization has hit a peak. Things become consistent and not just an up and down rollercoaster. This is your place of breakthrough, your place of SUCCESS!

For a leader to acquire the last stage of **HAPPENS**, they must endure the entire process of the **P.U.S.H.** Everyone wants the big break, but no one allows the process to shape them for the big break. Someone once told me, "your gift can get you there, but your character will keep you there". This means just because you achieved success, doesn't mean you will keep it. It takes good character, and strong willed discipline and determination to achieve success.

> **PAUSE:** What does P.U.S.H look like in your life? In what area do you need improvement?

_____

_____

_____

_____

_____

_____

Stinkin Thinkin

Your mind is the first battlefield of your life. If you fail in your thinking, you will inevitably fail in life. Many times people fail in the area of self-discipline because they have "Stinkin Thinkin". They have already given up mentally, which causes them to give into various temptations and bad habits physically.

I used to possess "Stinkin Thinkin", to no fault of my own. My stinkin thinkin was influenced by my environment and by those who raised me. While growing up, I developed many bad habits, such as bad eating, bad spending, and bad understandings of money. I was taught things like you must get a job to survive and work until you can't work anymore. These bad habits started manifesting early in my life in my weight, my spending habits, and my business. I have struggled with my weight for most of my life, losing here and gaining there. I have struggled with my spending, by buying on impulse rather than logic. And I have struggled with knowing my value and worth, because I didn't have a job, I had a business that wasn't meeting the needs of my households. Due to these areas of my life I felt insecure and less than a man.

Now don't get me wrong, my family is great and I wouldn't trade them for the world. However, I understood that in order for me to get to my next level in life, I might not need to trade them, but I would have to trade their habits. These habits are similar to the ones many people grow up with, but the difference between being mediocre and being successful is understanding how not to be bound to broken systems.

Many people get caught in the trap of just living to get by; while being able to only sustain themselves and their families. But I made a conscious decision that I didn't just want to get by; I wanted to thrive and for me to do that my thinking would have to shift dramatically. Changing the way in which you think will inevitably change the way you live.

After seeing my life spiraling in a constant cycle, I decided then, and there something had to change. I had to get rid of my "Stinkin Thinkin". I began to read books of people who were already where I wanted to be. I began to attend seminars and presentations. I began to work on me. I focused on my personal development in order to not only become the best leader, but the best me I could be. Before you can become anything for anybody else, you first must become "it" for yourself. I destroyed my old system and embraced a new philosophy for my life. One that would not only sustain my life, but one that would allow it to thrive. Discipline allowed me the opportunity to do this.

Through discipline in reading, discipline in eating, and discipline in my thinking, I was able to alter the course of my life and place myself on a trajectory to success. Many people are waiting for someone to help them change their life, but change must first start with you.

> **PAUSE:** What "Stinkin Thinkin" do you need to change in your life NOW? What new systems and habits should you replace them with?

_____

_____

_____

_____

_____

_____

Leaders that are successful in their careers, businesses, or organizations understand that what got you **HERE** won't get you **THERE** because if it could, you would already be **THERE**. **HERE** is where you are right now, and **THERE** is where you want to be. To get **THERE**, you have to let go of what you think is right **HERE** and adopt what people are doing **THERE**.

I had a coaching client who paid me top dollar to sit down and have a session with me. In this session, I began to give them strategies, plans, and processes to implement in their life and business that would allow them to achieve what they wanted out of life. After spending about an hour **POUR**-ing into this individual, they said something that infuriated me and that was, "I like the way I do it now."

They went on about how their husband gave them

this strategy; their family gave them this idea, and their kids helped them come up with this name for their business. They were so emotionally tied to old unreliable systems and bad habits that they almost didn't let them go. And I told them at that moment after calming down and collecting my thoughts, "You can stay **HERE** or go **THERE**." You can keep these emotional connections to old broken systems and be just like the system, **BROKE (HERE)**; or you can adopt successfully proven systems and make money **(THERE).** Guess which one they chose.

Many times in life we are too emotionally connected to processes, systems, and even people that do not work and ultimately hold us back. We carry this dead weight around our entire lives never noticing how heavy our load has become because of it. **LET IT GO!** Stop holding onto the old, and press into the new. Develop a strategy of discipline, stick to it and change your "Stinkin Thinkin."

- - - - - - - - - - - - - - -

> **PAUSE:** How does you're HERE look? How does your THERE look? And what do you need to do to get THERE?

_____

_____

_____

_____

_____

_____

_____

Practical Steps to Become More Disciplined NOW!

Many people always ask me what can I do right **NOW** to get headed in the right direction with my business, leadership skills, or organization. So let's discuss some practical tools and processes that you can implement **NOW** that will help you in the process of becoming more disciplined.

Goals

You should have 7-day, 30-day, 90-day, 180-day, and 365-day goals written out so that you can measure where you are, and see if you actually met those goals within the allotted time. If you don't have this, you are doing a disservice to yourself, and you are not serious about achieving your dreams. Individuals who are serious about achieving their dreams keep track of their progress towards those dreams. Without a way to measure your progress, you have no map to progress in the direction in which you are desiring to go.

"Any DREAM that is not MEASURABLE does not EXIST"

PAUSE: What are your goals for this month and this year?

_____

_____

_____

_____

_____

_____

Schedule

A schedule is not just a chore, it is a necessity. I have found many times that most individuals lack discipline, structure, and order simply because they lack a schedule. Schedules are an accurate, measurable tool that you can use to see where you are in regards to discipline and reaching your goals. If you are not completing what is on your schedule, then you are not disciplined and neither are you meeting your goals. *(Schedules should be no less than 30-day increments, and the next 30-day schedule should be created 7 days before its start)*

Consistency

Consistency is the key to discipline. Habits take 21 days to break and 7 days to form. Implement 2 new habits every week and stay consistent with them. Perform these habits every day at the same time for one week and then continue them from then on. If you want to see the change, you must be consistent.

"Change must always be balanced with some degree of consistency"

- Ron D. Burton

Commitment

Commitment is necessary for your dream to thrive. Anything you want to last, you must be committed to it. Husbands must be committed to their wives or their relationship will not last (and they will end up 6 feet under, or at least that's what my wife says). CEO's must be committed to their organization, or the organization will fail. Even kids must be committed to their work, or their grades will fall. All of these scenarios have something in common; without commitment failure is inevitable. You must be disciplined enough to stay committed even when it's uncomfortable. This leads me to my next practical step.

Be COMFORTABLE with Being UNCOMFORTABLE

Discipline requires that you stay the course even when the going gets rough. You cannot quit being consistent and committed just because you experience discomfort on the road to success. Every successful leader has experienced some form of discomfort, but because they overcame it, they were able to be great. Remember if you're comfortable you are dead; if you are uncomfortable, that means you're still living.

Overcome your Emotions

To be disciplined, you have to overcome your emotions. Leaders and successful individuals understand that they cannot be emotional in their decision making. Many times people are undisciplined, and never reach their dreams nor lead in the correct manner, because they live by their emotions rather than by logic. Emotional leading and decision making will eventually become detrimental because rather than rationalizing, you are emotionalizing, which leads to irrational choices.

Kick out the BUT's

You have to kick out the **BUT's** in your life and get off your butt (posterior) so that you can achieve a more disciplined lifestyle. **BUT's** are excuses that individuals make to keep them from being disciplined, causing them to feel better about their slothful progress in achieving their dreams. **BUT** stands for *"Believing Unknown Threats"*. This would imply that you are becoming afraid and fearful of progress due to the unknown. Many people kick their butts (posterior) right out of success because they are so consumed with fear of the future, that they make excuses for the present, and keep themselves bound to the past.

> **PAUSE:** What BUT's (excuses) have you made that have halted your progress to success?

_____

_____

_____

_____

_____

_____

_____

You have to define your *Why*

or your **mission** will always be a

DREAM

and will never **manifest** into

reality

CHAPTER 3

The Mission

What is a Mission?

Before we can talk about defining your mission, we first must know what a mission is. Mission is the why and vision is the how. The mission is what you want to achieve and why you want to achieve it. It is the backbone of every organization, entrepreneur, dream, and idea. Without a mission not only do you not know where you are headed, but you don't even know why you are going there. Many organizations and leaders I have worked with falter for this very reason. They lack the what, which means they possess no direction; and they lack the why which means they have no momentum.

If a ship was sailing on an ocean, the two things that are of necessity to the voyage are the map and the momentum (*what propels the ship forward*). Without these two items, the ship will not leave port. If the ship left without the map, not only would it have no direction, but no purpose. If the ship left port without momentum, it would have no way of navigating its course on the sea and would be taken away by the wind and currents. But it amazes me how many organizations, entrepreneurs, and leaders leave port without these two necessities. They don't know where they are going or how to get there, and they have no means of momentum and navigation that would allow them to be taken away by currents and stray winds. These individuals and organizations are winging it, instead of flying it. They are leaving port hoping things work out instead of actually having a set plan (*mission*) and strategy (*vision*) to get them where they are headed. It is imperative that organizations aren't just prepared, but equipped for the goals they want to achieve and the people they want to impact.

WHAT?

The **WHAT** of the organization/leader is literally the direction in which they are heading. It is the X on the map that marks where the treasure is. If they are missing the **WHAT**, then they have no direction and lack a sense of purpose. Without the, **WHAT** purpose can never be realized, and goals can never be achieved.

Every organization and leader needs to know their purpose; their **WHAT**. An organization without purpose is like a Quarterback who has no aim and throws without intention, without direction, and without vision. This type of throw usually leads to incomplete passes, lost yards, interceptions, and possibly even a touchdown for the other team. As leaders, we cannot afford to be like that Quarterback. When the team is depending on you to make the throw and win the game you cannot let them down by frivolously throwing the ball. You have to have some sort of direction, insight, and purpose behind your throw in order to complete the pass and make the touchdown.

I believe that is just how reality is; we must know our **WHAT** so that in our businesses, organizations, and lives we are throwing with a purpose. If we make business, organizational, or life decisions without the proper aim, we can expect something detrimental to occur, that it could cost us major losses in those areas. We have to gain focus on our **WHAT** so we can throw the ball with confidence and accuracy in the direction in which we wish to go. Remember as a leader you are the Quarterback and the team is depending on you to make the right calls.

PAUSE: What is your WHAT (purpose) for your business, organization, or life? In what direction are you trying to take those you lead?

_____

_____

_____

_____

_____

_____

WHY?

One day in a workshop I was hosting, I had a talk with some industry leaders, and we discussed their missions. Many of them knew their what. They knew what they wanted to achieve, what they wanted to make (money), and what they wanted to have. But it amazed me how many of them did not know their **WHY**. **WHY** do you want to achieve this, **WHY** do you want to make this amount of money, and **WHY** do you want to have a certain thing (i.e., buildings, employees, cars, etc.)? Many of them could not answer the question of **WHY**. So I asked them **WHY** should I help you? And the room got quiet.

Although they possessed the **WHAT**, they lacked the **WHY**, and it is the **WHY** that gives you substance. When speaking to them, I told them that they could tell people **WHAT** all day long, but that's not **WHAT** moves people. **WHAT** will move someone to invest in you financially, emotionally, and physically is your **WHY**.

Leaders must know the **WHY** behind the **WHAT** or else the **WHAT** means nothing.

Consider this scenario:

'An organization holds a massive meeting with all of its employees. The CEO stands up and says, "We want you to work harder to bring in more money for the company" and then sits down. 'Crickets.'

After hearing this how would you feel? Well, I don't know about you, but I would consider moving jobs. Obviously, this company doesn't care about its employees. The only thing they seemed concerned with is lining their pockets with more cash. Well, at least that's how it seems. Now let's consider the same scenario, but with the **WHY** added in:

An organization holds a massive meeting with all of its employees. The CEO stands up and says, "We are so proud of the work you have already done. But we would encourage you to work harder to sell more life insurance so that we can impact more families and help alleviate some of their burdens during an already stressful time. 'And the Crowd Goes Wild"

Wow! Talk about a dramatic change. Same setting and same timing, but a more defined mission. Your **WHY** is important! Yes, all companies want more money, let's be honest, but that is not what's going to move people to invest their money, time, or energy into what you are selling. It is the **WHY** that will move them to invest and possibly even partner with your mission. You have to define your **WHY** or your mission will always be a dream and will never manifest into reality.

> "Remember people are moved by your WHY, not your WHAT"

PAUSE: What is your WHY? How are you implementing your WHY to gain you more investment (time, energy, and of course money) regarding your dreams?

_____
_____
_____
_____
_____
_____
_____

WHEN?

Beyond your **WHAT** and **WHY** you must also possess a strategic plan that maps out the timing of **WHEN**. Knowing **WHEN** is just as critical as **WHAT** and **WHY**, because it gives you a time frame in which certain things should take place, and when tasks should be accomplished. A friend of mine, Jeff Dousharm of Paradigm Impact Group, made a great statement once. He said,

"People who say time is money don't understand what time is really worth"

-Jeff Dousharm

This quote stands to be true because time is the most valuable commodity known to man. You can't buy it, you can't sell it, and you surely can't own it (if anything it owns you). With that being understood, knowing your **WHEN** is not just important, it is critical for every dreamer, visionary, and leader. If you have goals you want to achieve, you must create a timeline in which you want to see those goals come to fruition. The longer you put off creating a timeline and knowing your **WHEN**, the more **TIME** you waste.

HASTE LEADS TO WASTE

In the process of preparing your **WHEN** (time-frames, time-lines, dead-lines, etc.), don't haste. Yes, time is valuable, but time well spent is even more precious. You have to make sure that you are not rushing the process of achieving your mission because *"Haste leads to Waste"*.

When we are young, we learn the meaning of this phrase from our parents. As a youth, my parents would say take your time on your assignments because you may miss something important. This statement proved to be very true. When I was in school, we had a test called the TAKS test or the "Texas Assessment of Knowledge and Skill." I always made "Commended" (90% or higher) on these tests, so I didn't take my time and rushed through them. When I would get the test back, I found out I always missed 2-3 questions, which kept me away from a perfect score. They were usually fairly simple questions, but they were worded in such a way that if you didn't pay attention, you would miss them. And guess what I did? That's right, you guessed it, I missed them. I missed these fairly simple questions not because I wasn't intelligent, but simply because I was going too fast, and not paying attention.

As I grew older, I learned the phrase "Haste leads to Waste" through my experiences. One such experience occurred during my graduate program, when an assignment was due. Because I hadn't yet caught the importance of the statement "Haste makes Waste", I rushed through the assignment. I thought I had more important matters to tend to, and that's where I was terribly mistaken. I ended up making a 72 on a major assignment, and though that might not seem bad in an undergraduate program, in a graduate program it is equivalent to failing. In the program I was in, you couldn't make less than around an 86 for the semester or you were dismissed (Kicked OUT).

This is when I got a true wake-up call and realized I could no longer rush through things in my life. It's not that you can't get by with rushing, it's that you will waste valuable time, energy, resources, and knowledge in the long run. "Haste makes Waste" and as leaders, we cannot afford to waste anything because we need everything to become fuel for the mission.

In the end, everything worked out for me, but I had to make up for the time I wasted through haste. I had to spend extra time and resources making sure I made perfect grades on my smaller assignments to make up for the haste on my larger one. Remember don't haste, because slow and steady wins the race.

PAUSE: What have you done hastily that has led to waste in your life? What will you do to stop being wasteful?

_____

_____

_____

_____

_____

_____

Stay Focused

Lastly, when creating your mission or pursuing it, remember that focus is key. Keeping your mind and mission focused are two very important components to becoming a successful leader. Leaders have to be focused mentally because if they are not, their judgments and decision-making skills will be cloudy; which could become detrimental to themselves and those they lead.

Take this into consideration. If the president of the United States, the most powerful individual in the free world, could not focus, what would be the results? The results would be catastrophic! Our army would not be coordinated, relationships with our allies would begin to falter, our enemies would see our weaknesses and attack, and I'm pretty positive World War III would begin. All of this would occur simply because the president was not focused.

Maybe you're not the president of the USA, and maybe World War III wouldn't start because you became unfocused, but think about what would happen in your family, organization, or life if your focus was not intact. A war would start, maybe not on the entire Earth, but surely in your world (your realm of influence). Your family would begin to implode, your organization would grow unstable, and your life would begin to fall apart. **FOCUS** is the glue that keeps everything together, and the key that unlocks the door to success in every area.

"Focus is critical for success concerning the mission"

"Cognitive control" is the scientific term for putting one's attention where one wants it and keeping it there in the face of temptation to wander. This focus is one aspect of the brain's executive function, which is located in the prefrontal cortex. A colloquial term for it is "willpower."

Willpower is needed for focus and necessary for leaders. Without willpower and focus, leaders will find it difficult to keep their eye on the prize. When I speak of an eye I am not speaking of one's physical eye; I am speaking of a mental eye or third eye if you will. This is the eye that holds the key to a leader's innate ability to be able to possess vision and insight that others don't have. Some call it ESP (extrasensory perception), some call it intuition, and some call it Prophetic, but for the sake of this book we are not going to get into this debate; all we need to know is that it is there and leaders need it. Without this third eye being able to envision where you are going is difficult and staying focused on that vision is almost impossible. Leaders have to possess the ability to see what others can't see, so that they can do what others can't do.

One of my favorite books is the Bible, and in 2 Corinthians 4:18 it says something very profound. It states, "While we look **_not_** at the things which are seen, but at the things which are not seen: for the things which are seen *are* temporal; but the things which are not seen are eternal." This verse is critical in the formation of a leaders focus in any religion, because it points out the importance of not getting caught up in what you see physically (natural), but instead to stay focused on your mission and dream which is metaphysical (spiritual).

In the end, leaders have to be focused, and to possess true focus you must have enhanced vision which can only be possessed when you look to the source which is within. For me that source is Jesus Christ, the messiah. To you that source may be something different, but to possess the vision it is imperative you find it.

PAUSE: How do you stay focused? What is your source for vision?

THE MISSION

"Many people choose individuals

they like at the expense of

WHAT and WHO

they need".

CHAPTER 4

Possessing an Effective Team

Why a Team?

I have had many leaders, entrepreneurs, and visionaries who were just starting off, ask me the question, "Why do I need a team?" Many of them think they can do everything themselves because that is what they have always done. Anytime you are entering into a new level of success, a team is critical to the process of obtaining it and thriving in it. Teams can make or break an individual or an organization because without the right team producing effective results, you will be ineffective in your goals and outdated in your approaches.

Possessing the right teams is necessary for success in leadership and organizations because they bring a level of insight and foresight that you may not have possessed otherwise. Many times team members allow you the luxury of new opinions and ideas that may lie outside the scope of your familiarity. These differing perspectives make teams an invaluable asset that every leader and organization needs in order to reach more people and make a bigger impact.

So the question should never be, "Why a team?" But instead, "Why not a team?" Teams make leaders and organizations look good because they are an extension of them and what they offer. Remember, you are only one person and you only possess two hands, two legs, and one brain; imagine what you could accomplish if you doubled, tripled, or even quadrupled that amount. I am positive a lot more could be accomplished, and more goals could be met and possibly even exceeded. The right team is the key to next level growth and success for leaders, businesses, and organizations; so know who is on your team.

— — — — — — — — — — — — —

PAUSE: Do you think teams are important? What could you accomplish with the right team?

_____

_____

_____

_____

_____

_____

The Football Team

In sports, teams are critical to obtaining the goal of winning games and achieving the mission, which is to become superior in their league; which is achieved specifically by winning super bowls, championships, etc. The specific sport that I want to highlight is that of football.

Football is America's sport and has been around since 1869. It is a sport that is deeply engrained into American society and impacts the nation at large when the season starts. In the movie 'Concussion', Albert Brooks makes an interesting statement, and says that Football owns a day of the week (Sunday). This statement proves to be true due to the Sport's massive popularity. Football is not a 1-man sport; it is a team endeavor. That is why you need the right individuals, in the right positions, at the right time for the team to be effective. In football, there are different positions that provide different functions to support the goal, which is winning a game, and assist in accomplishing the Mission, which is winning the Super Bowl.

What is critical to note here is that all 32 NFL teams have the same goal of winning games, and the same mission of winning the Super Bowl. But only 1 out of the 32 will achieve their mission, although all of them (hopefully) will achieve their goals at some point.

> **PAUSE:** What mission do you want to achieve that requires you to become superior to those you are competing against?

Let's look at some of the positions in football, their functions, and their relation to an effective team:

QB or Quarter Back:

First is the QB or (Quarter Back) who is the team captain. He throws and sometimes runs the ball. His objective is to **GUIDE** the team down the field to the goal line and inside the end-zone for a touchdown. To do this he has to be smart and cunning to out-maneuver the other team and find openings to throw the ball to the best individuals.

From a leadership perspective, this position would be the leader (CEO, Owner, Pastor, etc.). This is the head of the team that guides and directs them to the best routes, options, and decisions. They make sure they lead the team in achieving their goals and guide them to fulfilling the mission. They out-maneuver those who oppose their objectives and strategize as to the best course of action that should be taken in times of peace and distress.

Scorers:

Next, you have the Scorers who are the (Running Back/ Halfback, and Wide Receivers). These positions are responsible for scoring touchdowns and gaining yards. They, in a sense, are the workers on the team and the ones everyone depends on to help get them to their goals.

From a leadership perspective, these would be the top performers, managers, and usually those who have high ranking positions of authority. They are the ones that are pushing the team and even sometimes the leader to get things done so that a goal can be met. They are usually energetic, very committed, and loyal. They are very glamorous on the team, and everyone knows them because of how well they perform and how much they help in the process of achieving goals and fulfilling the mission.

Protectors:

Then you have the protectors, these are the positions that belong to the offensive line, and protect the Quarterback and the Scorers. Their primary function is to make the quarterback's job easy and the scorer's job possible. They make sure they are blocking the opposing team's tactics of trying to contain the quarterback, tackle the running back/half back, and block catches from the wide receiver. The protector's job is to make sure the quarterback is free, the running back has an open hole, and the wide receiver can catch the ball. These individuals protect the goals and mission of the team.

From a leadership perspective, these individuals are the ones who truly understand and are committed to the leaders/organizations mission and vision. They protect the leader and organization by being observant and watching for threats both internally and externally that may halt or slow down progression. They are usually the behind the scenes individuals and do the dirty work so that the mission may be realized.

Defenders:

Lastly, you have the defenders these are those who belong to the defensive squadron such as (Defensive Lineman, Linebackers, cornerbacks, and safety's). All of these positions provide different skills, but have the same function, which is to defend their end zone and stop the opposing team from scoring. They make sure that they stop the opposing team from gaining yards and touchdowns, through a variety of ways such as interceptions, tackles, blocks, etc. These are the hardcore men on the team.

From a leadership perspective, these individuals would be those who are up to date on new trends, techniques, and systems in the market. They make sure that they always have the upper hand on their opponents and help the leader to stay ahead of the game in their specific arena. These individuals are very observant and make sure that outside forces are not affecting internal functions.

PAUSE: Do you think that you accurately fit the position of Quarterback on your team? What could you do to improve your position as the leader?

_____

_____

_____

_____

_____

_____

Know What You Need & Who You Need

Leaders and organizations have to know the **2 W's** when it comes to choosing a team, and those **W's** are **What & Who.** You must know **WHAT** you need and **WHO** you need, or you will never possess an effective team. You have to know the **WHAT** before you know the **WHO.**

The **WHAT** are the things you're missing around you that you need on your team. Define your **WHAT**! Many leaders and organizations have not defined their **WHAT.** If you don't know **WHAT** you need you will never find **WHO** you need, and you will end up with something you don't need. Think about the different components of football we just talked about; the Scorers, Defenders, and Protectors. Know which areas you are missing and find people that can fill those positions that line up with your need.

Many people choose individuals they like at the expense of **WHAT** and **WHO** they need. This is leadership and organizational immaturity. As mature leaders we have to sacrifice our wants to take care of our needs. Sometimes our best friends or family members may not be the best choice for the positions that need to be filled. Loyalty that does not produce needs to be severed and replaced. Your loyalty cannot outweigh your need or else you will be unsuccessful. Being loyal to dysfunctional people, processes, and systems will be your consent to your own demise.

Lastly, don't settle for someone **WHO** is there. Many

leaders settle for people that are there instead of waiting on **WHAT** and **WHO** they need. The right people are around, but they will be harder to find than the average Joe because they are more effective. Don't fill a position on your team with someone who is not **WHAT** you need, and not **WHO** you want. Many organizations I have worked with have done this, and it has caused them **HELL**. Instead of waiting on the right people they chose candidates that were not qualified, nor had the experience for the position they were being placed in. And because they did not wait, these people caused them hell in the office, slowed down productivity in their sectors and others, and impacted their bottom line negatively. So yes, the position was filled; but being filled with crap never feels good.

DON'T SETTLE! You, your team, and organization are better than accepting someone that does not meet up to the standards that have been set. I know that seems harsh but it is true, and if no one has told you this already, you are better than who you are right now; and what you have right now. So don't settle for less than the best.

> **PAUSE:** Who is on your team and which position do they fit into? Who do you need on your team and what positions will they fill?

_____

_____

_____

_____

_____

_____

The Highest Commodity

People are not just important they are necessary and critical for any organization or leader to realize success. Many leaders and organizations fail because they undervalue the importance of a team, and are unconcerned with the wellbeing of those they serve. The primary definition of commodity is, "something or someone useful or valued". People are the highest commodity of any leader and organization because they not only bring in return, but reproduction. The return of something is based on what you put into it; but people don't just bring in return, they bring in skill, knowledge, gifts, talents, experience, and connections, which they then reproduce on your team.

All of these great attributes come with individuals that you bring on your team without you ever having to do anything extra. These attributes could take leaders and organizations to deeper depths of knowledge and skill; and to higher heights of success. But for this to be realized they must first see the valuable commodity they have in their possession. Furthermore, many leaders and organizations miss out on all of these great benefits not because they want to, but because they don't allow their team to **OWN** the mission. When someone takes ownership of something they in turn feel responsible for it. So, when leaders allow their teams to own the mission, the team is now partially liable for the completion of that mission. This means that team members will now do everything in their power to make sure that the mission is completed, because they are now responsible for it.

One of my mentors, Dr. Regina Spellmon, always says a quote by the famous Myles Munroe,:

"Where purpose is unknown, abuse is inevitable"

-Myles Munroe

This is seen over and over again on teams all around the world, because leaders and organizations refuse to see the value in the people they have. When you don't understand a person's true purpose you will never be able to put them in the right position, which causes you to view them simply as **ANOTHER**. I have seen this scenario many times in different organization and groups. Because they don't know the value of the individual they treat them like just **ANOTHER** worker, **ANOTHER** team member, or **ANOTHER** associate; without realizing fully what they have to offer.

A friend of mine was working for an organization that was having a few internal issues, and they needed some assistance. This particular organization did not possess the finances that it would cost to get the assistance they needed, but my friend possessed the connection, which was me. One night after work she was telling me about the issues her organization was facing. I then asked why she hadn't brought the issues to me sooner, especially since my company specializes in organizational development. She then said, "Oh don't worry about it; I would never use my personal connections to help them, especially with how they treat me there."

This organization could have had very discounted and possibly even free help if they only had known the value of the people they had in their organization. Sadly, this happens every day around the world because again; "Where purpose is unknown, abuse is inevitable". Due to them not seeing value in my friend, I didn't see value in helping this organization out. In the end, my friend found a better position and the organization she left shut down a few months later.

One connection could have saved their business and kept their doors open, but they did not know the valuable commodity they possessed.

> **PAUSE:** What do you think the quote by Myles Munroe means? "Where Purpose is Unknown abuse is inevitable?

_____

_____

_____

_____

_____

BUY-In

I firmly believe if the organization my friend was a part of had seen her value and had gotten her to **BUY-In** to their mission, she would have released the connection she possessed with me, which could have saved the organization. People will not release all of their talents, gifts, connections, skills, and experiences unless they have a sense of ownership in the mission.

What does **BUY-In** mean? It means that you are allowing them the opportunity to get emotionally, mentally, physically, and possibly even spiritually involved with the organization's mission. You are making them feel like they have ownership in the success and failure of the mission. Think about this:

The owner of an organization never wants to see that orga-

nization fail. They want the organization to succeed because it is a reflection of them, and many times, their livelihood.

This is the same thinking and philosophy that is used with the **BUY-In** method. You are allowing them to feel so connected with the mission that they have bought into the company without actually purchasing or possessing stock. They want to see the company succeed and thrive, because they feel that it is a reflection of them, their work, their time, and their emotions.

Great company's like Google and Apple understand this Method, which is why they do so much for their employees. They understand that to make customers **BUY-In** their staff and team must first **BUY-In** to the mission, vision, and product. **BUY-In** is critical when you want to increase productivity and expand an organization. Remember team members will only release their full potential when they have bought into the mission.

PAUSE: What will you do to help your team BUY-In to your mission and be committed to your or your organization?

_____

_____

_____

_____

_____

_____

"TEAMS will only be developed to the extent of their **leader's development** and will only be committed to the development process at the **depth of their buy-in**".

CHAPTER 5

Developing the Team

Leaders can possess a team, but if the team is not developed, they will by result be ineffective. Many leaders and organizations deal with this problem because their team members possess talent, but the talent is ineffective because it is underdeveloped. Think about this. Just because I am a broker does not mean I am effective at being a broker in every arena. There are hundreds if not thousands of different types of brokers operating in different arenas, trying to close different contracts and deals. This means that if I am a real-estate broker, I might not perform well trying to create, find, and close deals in the entertainment industry because, even though I have the skill, I might not be developed in that specific field.

When working with leaders, I always tell them "an undeveloped team will leave you ineffective in your industry, impact your bottom line negatively, and cause you more hell than their talent can afford." This means that a team that is not fully ingrained in your industry and does not have an understanding of where you are headed will begin to hold you back instead of propel you forward. As a leader you cannot just have a team, you have to also be committed to developing that team individually as well as corporately.

Teams will only be developed to the extent of their leader's development and will only be committed to the development process at the depth of their buy-in. If leaders refuse the development process, they will not only halt themselves but their team. Furthermore, if they neglect to develop those that follow them they are also neglecting the success that could be gained from the process of development.

PAUSE: What does this quote mean to you?: "an undeveloped team will leave you ineffective in your industry, impact your bottom line negatively, and cause you more hell than their talent can afford".

_____
_____
_____
_____
_____
_____

The Importance of POUR-ing

Leaders and organizations all around America miss the importance of **POUR**-ing, which stands for *"Pushing Out Undesired Restraints"*. I'm sure you're asking yourself right now, what in the heck does that mean? Well, let me explain. It is the leaders job to push out anything that is restraining them, their team, or their organization from completing goals and achieving the mission. Any obstacle that the team is facing, now becomes the leader's responsibility. With that responsibility comes the task of having to remove the restraints so that the team can freely progress and not be hindered by what was once holding them back.

Because many leaders don't see their team member's problems as their problems, they refuse to accept this ideology and revoke the process of **POUR**-ing. The process of *"Pushing Out Undesired Restraints"* is one in which every leader needs to make sure they are committing themselves to, because if the team is held back so are they. The issue with many leaders and organizations is that they are selfish in their ambition and arrogant in their pursuit, which in the end, will lead to them never achieving their goals.

Successful leaders and organizations understand that to stay successful they must have a team that can weather the storms that they will indeed face on their journey. The only way to weather that storm is to push out any restraints that may be holding that team back. So stop and think, what is holding you, your team, or your organization back from achieving goals and completing the mission? And secondly, what are you doing about it?

Great leaders become great because they not only see problems, but also find solutions to those problems. More than half of organizational failures occur because of internal breakdowns, and more than anybody, leaders are responsible. You have to make time to develop your team. Chuck Yeager said,

"There's no such thing as a natural-born pilot."

– Chuck Yeager

This insinuates that no one is born ready; everyone has to be developed into what they are to become. As leaders, it is our responsibility to take the time necessary to assist those who are under our guidance in the process of becoming all that they can be and not be held back by restraints.

> **PAUSE:** What is holding you, your team, or your organization back from achieving goals and completing the mission? What are you doing about these restraints?

_____
_____
_____
_____
_____
_____

The DEVELOPMENT Process & Investment

So I'm sure you're asking, "What is the development process?" "How does that look?" and "When should it be implemented into my team?" Well, let's talk about it. Firstly, the development process is different trainings and coaching that you send your team through so they can learn more and so that you may gain a larger investment back from what you have **POUR**-ed into them.

The process of team development is just that, a **PRO-CESS**. It requires that you invest into your team first before you ever see a return. Many leaders fear this process because they feel that they might lose the investment they are putting in. They fear things like the team member being uncommitted to the process, or the team member leaving with the knowledge, resources, and time that was poured into them. These are legitimate concerns, and I would be lying if I told you that it's not possible for these scenarios to occur, but there is a way to avoid this turmoil altogether. What if I told you there is a secret to making sure that your investment doesn't go to waste, and a way to receive the biggest return on those who you are investing in? I'm sure right now you are thinking, "I would love to know this supernatural method to avoid chaos, and gain success." Well, the answer is, 'get them to buy-in first', and gain commitment second.

What do I mean? Well, we talked about the **Buy-In** process earlier, so you understand how that process looks and works. Now you have to see at what level has their **Buy-In** caused them to commit. Why have they bought into your vision, or the company's mission? You have to find out what makes them tick. Find out what made them commit to you and what will keep them committed.

Let's look at a few different types of Commitment levels you will encounter:

Are they committed due to money?

Because if they are, you know they are not committed to your vision any more than what your vision can offer them financially. This means that when the money stops rolling in, they will stop rolling in; or if your competitor beats your price they will steal your investment. These individuals are seasonal individuals. You shouldn't invest too much into them because they are not deeply invested in your mission or you. So that means you gain what you need from them and let them move on. You only give these types of individual's expendable jobs and not long term positions.

Are they committed due to emotional attachments?

Some people don't choose jobs because of money some choose them because of emotional attachments. Maybe their grandma was a nurse, so they desired to become one. Maybe they always had a dream of being a veterinarian since they were a child. Or maybe they love helping kids. You or your organization might offer them the opportunity to do these things. These are emotional attachments that they correlate with their position and because of this, these individuals will support you as long as you are supporting their emotional attachment. They will be committed to you so long as you are committed to their emotional desires in that position or until something better opens up for them. These individuals don't have a **BUY-In** to the vision more so than how the vision meets their emotional wants, desires, and needs. These individuals can be offered lengthier term positions, and can be invested into more because, though they aren't the safest investment, you are offering them a place on a team they desire to be a part of. The desire they have to meet their emotional attachment needs, will cause a decent level of commitment, and a return on your investment.

Are they committed to the mission?

These individuals were sold on what you or the organization was doing after they heard your **"WHAT"** and your **"WHY"**. They are not worried about money, and their emotional attachment is not an outward influence more than it is an internal pull because, they have made a connection to you and your mission. They are attached to you, what you are doing, and where you are headed. They believe in the mission, believe it's possible to achieve, and believe they are supposed to be a part of it. These individuals deserve positions of leadership and authority due to them having you and your mission's best interest in mind, which they feel is also their best interest. They deserve to be **POUR**-ed into more and deserve more of your personal time because they are giving more of themselves to you.

After you figure out what commitment level they possess then, you can begin to invest in them accordingly. You only invest in team members at the level of their **BUY-In** and commitment.

How to Invest

Now let's talk about how to invest and what that process looks like for a team. Many teams are underdeveloped not because the leaders or organizations don't want to develop their teams, but because they simply don't possess the wherewithal to do it. Many leaders and organizations feel that they lack the time to invest in their teams properly; others think they lack the resources, and some think they can't teach what they don't know themselves. Again these are legitimate concerns, but there are practical steps that every leader and organization can take tomorrow to begin the process of team development.

Books

Reading books is one of the quickest and easiest ways for leaders and organizations to begin the process of growth and development in their teams. Books are cheap and usually can be purchased for discounted prices if bought in bulk. To get the entire team on one page you can purchase multiple copies of one book and have the whole team read it. This can be your way of implementing corporate growth. This is the area in which those you don't want to invest too much in have the opportunity to participate in the development process. With books, you can also be more personalized with the development process because instead of buying one corporate book, you could buy multiple books that are personalized to each individual's growth. This is a great process, especially for those who you want to invest more in and will benefit from the readings you are offering them. Remember, there are millions of books on millions of subjects, so what you and your team need is out there if you search.

Events

Events such as seminars, workshops, and trainings are another great way to take those on your team from zero's to hero's in a short time frame. These events vary in their cost and time lengths. There are some that can range from free - $1,000,000+ and some can take 1hr while others are over a month. You have to figure out how much money and time you are willing to invest in your team to get them to their next level of productivity, morale, and success. These types of events are offered in various places by different coaches, groups, and organizations. Some of my favorites are of course Empowerment Coaching, Sprinklism's Inc., John Maxwell events, and Tony Robinson's seminars. I believe attending these events, and participating in these trainings with your team will increase their morale, hone their focus, develop them as leaders, and make them more productive. Events and trainings are a quick and effective way to develop your team.

Meetings

Many leaders and organizations miss the effectiveness of meetings. Everyone downplays what a meeting can do for the team and the benefits it provides for everyone to be on one accord in regards to the mission and vision of the leader or organization. Meetings are very undervalued because they are not held in an effective fashion. Try changing the scenery of your meetings and get your team involved; go to a bowling alley, play a round of golf, ride go-carts, or watch something informative yet entertaining. Changing your scenery and developing interpersonal ties, while also stimulating their bodies and changing their minds about meetings, will increase the effectiveness of what is heard, maintained, and performed after the meeting.

These are practical tools that can be implemented on your team **NOW** which can drastically redirect you from an ineffective route to a successful course. Remember, due to one's slothfulness in implementing change; you will deny yourself the benefits of the results of that change. As I said earlier in the book, don't be committed to old systems that have failed to produce effective results. **CHANGE** is good, but it is **UNCOMFORTABLE**. Discomfort will last only a moment but from it, sustained success can be attained.

PAUSE: What steps can you implement NOW that can drastically impact the course of where your team is headed?

_____

_____

_____

_____

_____

_____

Create a Legacy Plan

Every leader needs a legacy plan. They need a plan that they have created that revolves around the process of creating more leaders. Tom Peters once said,

"Leaders don't create followers; they create more leaders."

— **Tom Peters**

Although the above quote is true, I would tweak it just a bit, and would say, "Great leaders don't create followers, they create more Great leaders." Because leaders are a dime a dozen but great leaders are rare to find. Great leadership is only revealed when a leader can replicate themselves (skill, wisdom, knowledge, understanding, etc.) into those that follow them.

Legacy leaders do exactly as the name suggest, which is leave a legacy. They impart their knowledge, skill, wisdom, understanding, and systems into those that follow them and are able to recreate leaders in the process. These new leaders then either take over the vision of the leader/organization or start their own mission. They then begin to replicate themselves into others, which in turn makes the first leader a legacy leader. Legacy leaders leave such an imprint on the lives and hearts of those they touched, that the new leaders begin to teach and pour into others the way that they poured into them.

Legacy leaders also set themselves up for success just in

case anything ever happens to them. If your business cannot function without you, you did not create a business you created a job. Implementing the best systems and making sure that those who follow you can comprehend and implement those systems without you is legacy leadership. Your mission and what you have created should not die when you die. As a legacy leader, you should have created systems in both the business and the people you serve, that can sustain and propel the mission in your absence.

Legacy leadership is about more than just creating a retirement plan for yourself although it does help in that area. It's about impacting generations of leaders by correctly **POUR**-ing into and developing those that are under your guidance. Legacy leaders are concerned with those they lead and how they lead them, because they know that they will one-day lead someone.

PAUSE: Do you have a Legacy Plan? If so, What and Who is your legacy plan? If not, what will it look like when it is created?

_____

_____

_____

_____

_____

_____

The Law of the Lid (John Maxwell)

Many of you may know and some may not know about the "Law of the Lid". But I thought it was critical to discuss it in regards to this conversation concerning team development. I believe John Maxwell's the "The Law of the Lid" is important to understand for every leader that is pursuing, or is in the process of developing their team. So for those who don't know I am sure you are asking the same question I was before I read John Maxwell's book and that is, "What is the Law of the Lid?" and "How does it affect my ability to empower my team?". Let's talk about the importance of this leadership law.

Every leader has a level of leadership that they are on, and those levels range between 1-10. A leader that is at level 7 can only grow a team or organization to a level of 5 or 6. **WHY?** Because the success of the team or organization can never bypass the level of the leader, or else the leader will break under pressure while leading. I believe this is also true when you are developing your team. You cannot develop a team that is higher on the scale than you. It becomes an impossible task because there is nothing you can **POUR** into them. When the team or organization's level exceeds that of the leader's a change in position has to be made because a 10 will not follow a 6; and sometimes a 10 will not follow a 10 because that's what 9's are for.

Take a moment, stop and think about what level of leaders and skill sets you are attracting. What you consistently attract is a reflection of who you are and how you perform as a leader. Are you attracting 2's and 3's? Well, that may mean you are a 4. Evaluate yourself and those around you.When individuals are searching for leadership, they desire someone they can look up to, not someone who they see eye to eye with or can look down upon. With that being said, be aware of your level of leadership in the process of developing your team. Are you a 1, or are you a 10. If you are anything below a 10 you need to start becoming more committed to the process of personal development so you can raise your lid and attract the level of leaders and skill sets that you desire on your team. Remember this quote from John Maxwell's book 'The 21 Irrefutable Laws of Leadership',

"Personal and Organizational effectiveness is proportionate to the strength of" leadership".

-John Maxwell

> **PAUSE:** Evaluate your what skill levels and levels of leaders you attract? What is your leadership level? What can you do to raise the lid on your leadership abilities?

Casting the VISION

and building relationships takes time that *many choose not to invest*, which is the reason for their *failure at achieving their goals.*

CHAPTER 6

Casting the Vision

As we know Great teams are not just important, they are imperative for all leaders, bad, good, great, or otherwise. If any leader ever wants to achieve anything they will need a good team. Great leaders understand the importance of having a trustworthy team to fulfill the mission and execute the vision. Without a great team, it is impossible to be a great leader because you have nothing to lead.

Great leaders choose people who are able to understand where they are going and people who will be committed to the journey. Leaders have to take the necessary time to find not just a good team but the right team. I say this because a team can be good but not right for the job, nor for where that leader is headed. Investing time, energy, and resources to find the right team is imperative especially when a leader is trying to go to the next level and achieve success.

A leader must take time to invest in the team they have. If a leader does not invest time into building relationships and casting the vision; while also giving direction, instruction, and correction then their team will begin to fall apart. Great leaders understand that they are the visionary which means they hold the vision and have to disperse it properly and effectively so that those they lead are able to catch it. Casting the vision and building relationships takes time that many choose not to invest, which is the reason for their failure at achieving their goals.

Casting the Vision requires that you first understand your vision and know your **"HOW."**

— — — — — — — — — — — — — —

PAUSE: How does a great team correlate with your vision and mission? What do you have to invest into your team as a leader so that they can be prepared for the mission and vision?

_____

_____

_____

_____

_____

_____

Define your "HOW"

To gain more followers and to impact the followers you already have, you will have to define your **"HOW"**. After you have explained your **"WHY"** and **"WHAT"** as we discussed earlier in the book, people will want to know **"HOW."** What plans, systems, processes, and strategy's do you have in place to complete your mission? When you show people **"HOW"**, it encourages them, because they are not believing in something that seems impossible, they are believing in something you have given them a strategy to achieve. Yes, seeing is not always believing, but to believe you must have an understanding of what you believe in. Possessing no understanding of what it is that you are standing on makes it impossible for you to stand firm.

"HOW" is your plan or vision that you will implement

to accomplish the mission. Without the **"HOW"** people might believe in the **"WHAT"** and **"WHY"** but will not be able to produce action behind it, because you have not offered them a plan of execution. Strategy and execution are essential to any mission and are critical to obtaining success. Strategy gives a map or game-plan on where to go, what to do, and when to do it. This affords those that follow you the opportunity to prepare, plan, and produce when necessary.

Leaders and Organizations fail in this area because many people think that a job description is a game plan. Yes, it is part of the **"HOW"** but it is nowhere near the full plan, and no one can execute the **"HOW"** successfully with only a job description. Those you lead have to understand the full scope of the vision and then you can break their specific functions down from there. If you only give someone a job description, they will not understand how their role plays a part of significance in the scope of the overall vision. They will also not understand the importance of their roles to other roles, which will lead to dysfunction, breakdown in communications, and afflicted team morale.

Your team and organization needs to know the **"HOW"** so they can be committed to the process that will have to be endured in order to achieve the mission. The **"HOW"** is the last selling point of the mission, because if people think the **"HOW"** is too hard and unattainable, they might change their minds about being on board with the mission. But if they see that the **"HOW"** is challenging yet achievable, it will make them more motivated to stay committed to what they believe in. Make sure you define your **"HOW."**

> **PAUSE:** What is your "HOW" (strategy, plan, course-of-action) for your mission?

_____

_____

_____

_____

_____

_____

Explain the Vision Clearly

After you have clearly defined your **"HOW"**, you have to clearly explain it to those who are on your team or in your organization. This is usually where there is a breakdown in communication from the leader to the team because it is done incorrectly and inconsistently.

When explaining your **"HOW"** one of the first things you must keep in mind is that everyone does not think like you. In my time of training leaders, I believe this is the hardest thing for many of them to understand. They think once they have the mission and vision, and explain it to people, that the people will get it immediately. Remember you are the visionary, which means you possess all of the information on the **"WHAT," "WHY"**, and **"HOW."** As a leader, you have to keep in mind that even though you have all the information, you are transferring all of that to people who know nothing about it. This means you have to be careful of what you say, how you say it, and when you say it.

Remember, as a leader you have a very special mind and think very differently from others. Your mind is always 10 steps ahead of where the team or organization is, and you cannot talk to them from that far ahead of them, or the information you give them will become diluted and misconstrued. As a leader, it is your responsibility to bring yourself down to their level so they can understand from their point of view. Keep in mind they are not on the mountain top, you are; so sometimes you have to come down and communicate on the ground level where they are. Yes, it's hard but as a leader, it is your duty.

- - - - - - - - - - - - - - -

PAUSE: How do you communicate to your team, from the mountain or on their level? What can you do to improve your communication?

_____

_____

_____

_____

_____

_____

_____

Knowing how to communicate properly and effectively is another issue for many leaders, believe it or not. This is because they are so excited about the new found revelation they have received and share that information out of place and out of time. This does more harm than good because it leaves those who they released the information to confused and in distress. This is due to the fact that they have just received new information on the mission or vision they didn't know before, and they don't know how to process it. Team members want to make sure they are doing the right thing, and when you give information to the wrong people, in the wrong setting, and at the wrong time, you place them in a very vulnerable position. They don't know what to do with what you have just given them. Many times they feel that because you told them there is an expectation for them to line up with this new information. You have just put more stress and worry on a team member than was necessary, because you gave them good information, but at the wrong time.

One time, when working with an organization in Texas, the leader and I sat down together and had a meeting about the direction in which they were headed. This meeting brought him clarity and new fresh ideas. This was an awesome experience for him because questions he had been asking for years had been answered in just one consultation. But when I left, what I didn't expect was for him to go and tell some of the lower level employees about what we had just discussed. This caused confusion in the organization because those who had less authority knew more than those who had higher positions. How would it make you feel if your subordinates came and told you critical information about the organization that you were not aware of? It would make you furious, right. Well, that is exactly what happened.

It caused **CHAOS** inside the organization and almost led to its destruction. This event led to major 'trust issues' within the leader's executive team. They felt betrayed that he would release critical information about the direction of the organization to lower level team members before they were ever informed. Members of the board were getting ready to vote the leader out, and others were considering resigning if he did not leave. This all happened simply because the leader was so excited that he released the right information, but at the wrong time, to the wrong people. This reveals that you must concern yourself with the way information is released, to whom it's released, and when it's released; so that you can protect those under your leadership.

In the end, 2 executive team members left, and others were angry but decided to forgive the leader because he had established relationships with them. But all of this could have been avoided if the leader had just been aware of how and when to release important information.

> **PAUSE:** What could the leader have done to better in this scenario?

_____

_____

_____

_____

_____

_____

The Order of Information Release

We have seen how important it is that information is released through the proper channels. So now let's talk about how and to whom information should be released, on any team or in any organization:

Leaders

After receiving any new found revelation, direction, or information concerning the mission or organization the first individuals that should be notified are the leaders. On many teams these leaders have multiple names; maybe they are the executive team, the board of directors, the assistant principals, the assistant pastors, and etc. Whatever those positions are called they should be the first to know about any information, big or small, that is going to be released to the rest of the team or organization. You have to remember that you are telling them because, yes, they hold authority in the organization, but also because they hold relationships with people you might not. Relationships and connections are key when new information or direction is released, especially when it drastically alters the course of where the organization is headed. Keep in mind that people don't like change, but they tend to better receive it when someone they like or respect is delivering that change to them. So leaders first.

Overseers/Managers

The second group that should be notified by you or the leaders should be those who are overseers in the organization. Now this group of individuals is composed of two different types of people; those who hold actual positions of authority and those who are influencers but may not hold a high rank. Bringing these two groups together and explaining the new information to them clearly is direly important, because they are usually the closest ones to the workers and volunteers. They usually have good interpersonal connections with people you may not even know the name of, which makes them critical to the release of information and casting the vision to the organization. This group of individuals are like the captains in the military who are over different squadrons; they are important and necessary for information to continue to flow down through the ranks.

Workers/Volunteers

The next group that should be informed are the workers. These are your individuals that may not have much authority, but they are also those who perform most of the critical work for the organization. Their voice is usually not heard alone, but instead echoes in numbers. They are the blood that keeps leaders' and organizations' missions alive. These individuals are like the foot soldiers in the army, and your main concern here is morale. If you can present the information in an effective manner, that increases their morale and changes their trajectory to realign with the new objective, you have done your job.

> **PAUSE:** Have you been releasing information through the right channels? What can you do to improve the way you release information to your team or organization?

_____

_____

_____

_____

_____

_____

HOW TO C.A.S.T

When casting the vision and releasing information to an organization, there is a model that I teach to those I coach, and it is an acronym for **CAST**, "**C**onsistently, **A**ffectively, **S**incerely, and **T**ransparently". The definition of cast is, to throw (something) forcefully in a specified direction. If we take this definition and apply it to a leadership model, it literally means to throw your mission, vision, or information forcefully in a specific direction so that the team or organization understands where you are headed.

Let's break down the acronym for **CAST:**

Consistently

When casting information one of the most important things you must do is be consistent. Consistency is the key to understanding. If you have ever had any formal education, then you understand this concept to be true. If you did not study something consistently you would forget it and fail a test; and the same is true in leadership. If you do not consistently place the mission, vision, or new information in front of those you lead, then they will forget it or believe it isn't important. Think about how much information people are presented with daily that you have to combat so that your information can sink in. You must be consistent for your information to be effective on the team or in the organization.

Affectively

As a leader when you are releasing information to your team or organization you must be affective. Affective is different from effective because the word affective speaks to the emotions of the individual. You must find ways to deliver new information about the mission, vision, or systems in a manner that impacts those you lead in an emotional way so that it can be more effective. Remember, if you are affective you will always be more effective, because what you have said now holds more weight due to its impact on their emotions. Emotions many times control decisions. Think about how many decisions you have made based on your emotions (I know that just brought up a few unpleasant memory's). I'm sure you have made a lot even if they weren't rational. The same thing goes for releasing information to teams; you can get them to make decisions you have already chosen beforehand, based on emotional appeal. Affectivity is essential and emotional appeal is critical when trying to communicate important information effectively.

Sincerely

When casting information as a leader what you are saying must come across as being Sincere. When delivering sensitive information that could change the course of the team or organization, it must be transferred with a sincere tone and heart. People want to know and need to know that you care, and that you have taken them into consideration with your decision. If people feel like you don't care you could have a potential problem on your hands, because they will begin to view you as a tyrant instead of a leader. Those that follow you need to know they can trust you; because, without trust, there is no connection and without connection, no mission can be accomplished. Every part of an electrical circuit must be connected so electricity can flow properly, and the same goes for an organization. If every part is not connected the propulsion you need to push the mission will not be able to function effectively.

Transparently

Lastly, as a leader, you have to be transparent. Stop trying to hold onto information that will have to be released later anyway. People want to know the truth up front, even if it doesn't feel good. Let them know what's going on, both good and bad, so that they can make a decision for themselves whether to stay on board the ship with you. Remember, if you communicate affectively then you will have effective results, even in the midst of your transparency. Don't hide from those you lead; they will respect you more if you are honest and upfront about what's going on.

PAUSE: What can you do to improve the way you CAST information to your team or organization? Do you think the CAST system will work for your team?

_____

_____

_____

_____

_____

_____

_____

CASTING THE VISION

SERVANT LEADERS

are *unique* because they don't look for people to give to them before they start *giving*.

CHAPTER 7

Servant Leadership

What is Servant Leadership

Being a servant leader will always be the highest form of leadership. Servant leaders are those who put the needs, wants, and desires of the individuals that follow them before their own. They are selfless individuals, and they give freely of themselves so that they can make sure their followers have everything they need, and when possible what they want. Servant leaders literally live to serve, and because they serve they find that it is easy to get people to serve them.

While servant leadership is a timeless concept, the phrase "servant leadership" was coined by Robert K. Greenleaf in The Servant as Leader, an essay that he first published in 1970. In that essay, Greenleaf said:

"The servant-leader is servant first... It begins with the natural feeling that one wants to serve, to serve first. Then conscious choice brings one to aspire to lead. That person is sharply different from one who is leader first, perhaps because of the need to assuage an unusual power drive or to acquire material possessions...The leader-first and the servant-first are two extreme types. Between them there are shadings and blends that are part of the infinite variety of human nature. "The difference manifests itself in the care taken by the servant-first to make sure that other people's highest priority needs are being served.

Servant leaders are unique because they don't look for people to give to them before they start giving. To be a great leader, you must be a servant leader, and you must always give first. Leadership requires that you give your time first, your thoughts first, your money first, and yes, sometimes you even have to give your heart (emotions) first. Leadership is all about giving first, and about being the one who has to sacrifice the most. Servant leaders are called to be sacrificial on teams and in organizations because they are the head, and being the head means that you have to look out for the rest of the body (organization).

PAUSE: What does the term "Servant Leadership" mean to you?

_____

_____

_____

_____

_____

_____

How does Servant leadership look?

Let's discuss the question, 'How does Servant Leadership look?' Well, servant leaders are all about the people. They are worried about the people's performance as well as their wellbeing, and will do anything within their power to make sure that those they lead are taken care of. Some examples of servant leaders would be people like Martin Luther King Jr. who put the needs of the African American people before his own well-being, and in the end gave his life for them fighting for their rights. Another would be Nelson Mandela who again, like Dr. King gave up his well-being and even found himself in prison fighting for equal rights for the people in South Africa. And lastly, a very famous servant leader can be found in the bestselling book in history, the Bible, in the form of Jesus Christ. Whether you believe in Jesus or not isn't the issue, but what cannot be denied is his contribution to servant leadership. He gave of himself and sacrificed for those who followed him, even unto the death of the cross. This means that he was so committed to his beliefs and to those who followed him that he would rather die than to allow the mission, and those following it, to perish and be put to shame. Jesus Christ was a true servant leader.

Now, we have looked at some great examples of servant leadership, but what do all of these great leaders have in common? Well, they all share the element of sacrifice. They gave so much of themselves that it eventually led to their deaths, imprisonment, or both. They chose to fight for what they believed in, even when adversity confronted them, and also to fight for the people they believed in, their followers.

Servant leaders lead in the face of great turmoil, confusion, and distress. They don't give up, and they surely don't give in because they know they have people depending on them to win. Servant leaders win not for themselves but for others so that they can share the sweet taste of victory with those that chose to follow them through the process. So we see that the answer to the question, "How does a servant leader look?" is, it looks like sacrifice.

> **PAUSE:** Who is an example of a "Servant Leader" in your life and why?

_____

_____

_____

_____

_____

_____

> *A research article by Stefano Ruggieri stated, "Leaders who display self-sacrificial behavior are considered by their followers to be more effective, charismatic, and legitimate than are self-benefiting leaders (Hoogervorst, De Cremer, van Dijke, & Mayer, 2012). Self-sacrifice involves the leader being willing to incur personal costs or run the risk of such costs to serve the goals and mission of the group or organization (Conger & Kanungo, 1987).*

Sacrificial Service

So, since servant leaders look like sacrifice let's discuss what that element really means to you as a leader. What is sacrifice? Sacrifice, as defined by Merriam-Webster is, "the surrender of something for the sake of something else". This would mean that sacrifice for servant leaders, is to give up something for someone else.

PAUSE: What have you sacrificed lately and for whom?

_____
_____
_____
_____
_____
_____

Leadership requires that the element of sacrifice be present in almost everything you do. As a servant leader, you must be ready to sacrifice at a moment's notice. I remember one day my beautiful wife and I were sleeping, and I received a phone call from one of my mentees in the middle of the night. I usually don't pick up my phone that late but for some reason, I truly felt led to do so. So I picked up the phone, and I heard panic in her voice; and as she breathed heavily, she began to describe to me the horrific occurrence that had just transpired. Her mother was in a bad accident and was on life support. As my wife and I began to speak to her and help her through the process of what had just happened she began to find peace and solace in knowing that there was hope for her situation.

I said all of that to say; servant leaders have to sacrifice when it is inconvenient. Convenience is not sacrifice. Sacrifice is the process of giving up something that you really don't want to give up for the sake of something or someone else. As a leader, you will be faced with many inconvenient situations and circumstances that will cause you to sacrifice, to overcome for those that you lead. Sacrifice doesn't feel good, heck, sometimes it's downright painful, but you have to push through the pain so that you can see the promise of your mission come to fruition.

Sacrifice is an element that every leader will have to come to grips with if they truly want to be successful. Success at anything, on any level, anywhere; will demand that you sacrifice something to achieve it. Success requires sacrifice.

PAUSE: Do you believe in the concept of sacrifice as a leader? Are you comfortable with sacrifice? What can you do to be a better servant/sacrificial leader to your followers?

Serve People and People Will Serve You

Did you know that serving your followers is one of the quickest ways to success? It's not an easy thing to do, but it is surely worth it because when you serve first, you will never be the last to be served. People will serve you easier and more effectively if you first serve them, because people love to know they are valued. Serving is a way of showing those that follow you they are valued and that you care about them. Serving first also shows that you value them beyond just what they can do for you, because before they have done anything you have already shown them appreciation through your service. How much more would you serve someone who has appreciated you before you have even produced results? I would hope your answer would be a lot. In the same way, that will also be your follower's answer to you, not in words, but in deeds.

People care about people who care about them, and people serve people who serve them; this is the law of reciprocity. Whatever you give will always return to you. Remember, just because it leaves your hand doesn't mean it has left your life.

As a leader, it is your job to make sure that your people are taken care of, not just financially but physically, emotionally, and in some cases spiritually also. Any leader that is not worried about the totality of the well-being of their followers will never become great. Servant leaders show interest in their follower's lives and do what they can to serve them to the best of their abilities in the areas where they are deficient. If you as a leader are not serving your follower's needs, you are lacking in service.

Great servant leaders know their followers needs many times before the follower ever can approach the leader with the need. Observation and connection to those you lead is a key to serving effectively. If you are not observant of those who are under your guidance, then you are not leading, you are managing. Managers are entirely different from leaders because they care about work, while leaders care about people. Being an observant leader and being able to see needs before they arise is one way of serving those who follow you. The other key to serving effectively is Connection. Leaders must be connected to make an impact because as one of my mentors Jonathan Sprinkles always says,

Points are Powerful, but CONNECTION IS KEY

-Jonathan Sprinkles

Why is connection key you ask? Because connection provides you access to your followers that you would not otherwise possess. Having connection and relationship with those you lead is a way of serving that makes them feel valued. Having interpersonal ties with your followers puts you in a position as a leader to be able to meet needs that may not have anything to do with work or the organization, but have everything to do with their performance. So your connection determines your reception. Remember, connection is literally the key to unlocking certain doors with those who follow you, which will allow you to gain access to things you may not have been able to gain before.

— — — — — — — — — — — — — —

> **PAUSE:** Do you believe Connection is Key as Jonathan Sprinkles so eloquently states? If so why? If not, why?

_____

_____

_____

_____

_____

_____

_____

S.E.R.V.E

Now that we have a good grasp of what a servant leader is and what one looks like, let's review **SERVE** in the form of an Acronym:

Sacrifice:

Remember servant leaders sacrifice for those who follow them. Sacrifice does not feel good and is usually never convenient, but leaders have to do it so that those they lead can have what they need. Sacrifice is one of the greatest forms of service that a leader can provide to a follower because it requires a leader to give up their wants, desires, well-being, and sometimes their life for those under their leadership. Sacrifice is necessary for success and is a critical element in the process of becoming a great servant leader.

Edify:

Servant leaders have to edify those under their authority. The word edify is defined as "the process of instructing or improving someone morally or intellectually. As a leader, it is your job to serve those under you by edifying them and making sure they have everything they need to succeed. Edification takes place when you begin to POUR into those under you and strengthen them in the areas in which they are weak. Great leaders take out time with their followers to help them grow so that they can become more effective in their positions, and personal lives. Servant leaders concern themselves with growing people, not businesses.

Reciprocate (reciprocity):

Servant leaders also give first which enables the law of reciprocity to activate. The law of reciprocity is simply explained like this, 'when someone gives you something you feel an obligation to give back.' As a leader when you give first in any manner you automatically invoke this law and what you give will return to you even if it is not from the same source you gave it to. Leaders cannot be stingy when it comes to giving because as a servant leader the process of giving is required. Giving first may hurt our pride, but many times, that is good because it brings us to a place of humbleness in our hearts. People like to serve people who have served them, and they also like to serve those who are humble. Remember the old proverb, pride comes before a fall.

Value:

Servant leaders value people, sometimes before they even deserved to be valued. True servant leaders understand that a person's worth is not in their ability or what they can do, but in the ability of who they can become. Great leaders have to be able to value what is inside people, even when the people cannot see it themselves. Leaders have to also value those they lead because when people feel valued and important they tend to be more productive, effective, and morale increases amongst colleagues. A valued follower is a productive follower because connection always comes before reception. If you want to receive the most from those under you, connect with them and value them.

Evoke:

Lastly, servant leaders evoke greatness from those that follow them. Evoke means, 'to bring out of, or draw out of'. The greatest leaders on earth are those who can make the invisible a reality, and can pull greatness out of individuals who don't even know they possess it. Many times leaders fail because they have what they need in their followers, but never evoke that need out of those they lead. As a leader, many times you will find individuals in your midst with hidden talents, or skills that they may not have known they possessed. These hidden skills may be exactly what you need, but if you don't see them and evoke them, they will stay just that, a hidden skill. Great leaders evoke greatness from their followers and in turn, produce great results in achieving their goals, missions, and aspirations.

= *SERVE*

Sacrificing, Edifying, Reciprocating, Valuing, and Evoking equates to the definition of serve. Serving is not easy; it's actually very difficult, and many times requires more than people are willing to give. But it is those who choose to sacrifice the most, that gain the most, and qualify for success. Leadership and Organizational success are always dependent on the depth of one's service.

PAUSE: What does SERVE mean to you? How has serving others impacted your life?

_____

_____

_____

_____

_____

_____

_____

Notes

Michael Jordan - Biography - IMDb. (n.d.). Retrieved from http://www.imdb.com/name/nm0003044/bio

"Lewinsky scandal - Wikipedia, the free encyclopedia.". N.p., n.d. Web. 09 Oct. 2016 <https://en.wikipedia.org/wiki/Lewinsky_scandal>.

2 CORINTHIANS 4:18 KJV "While we look not at the things ... (n.d.). Retrieved from https://www.kingjamesbibleonline.org/2-Corinthians-4-18/

Ruggieri, S., & Abbate, C. S. (n.d.). LEADERSHIP STYLE, SELF-SACRIFICE, AND TEAM IDENTIFICATION. 1171-1178. Retrieved October 9, 2016.

Greenleaf, R. (n.d.). The Servant as Leader. Corporate Ethics and Corporate Governance, 1-28. doi:10.1007/978-3-540-70818-6_6

Alford D. Simon is a dynamic teacher, author, minister, leadership expert, philanthropist, and Master Life Coach. He is the owner and CEO of Empowerment Coaching, Simon Ministries, and Co-owns Divine Desires with his wife, Taylor Simon. With over 10 years of experience in the Life Coaching industry, Mr. Simon has traveled across the country working with businesses, corporations, non-profit organizations, youth, and various school districts. As a heavily sought after motivational speaker, he is committed to seeing individuals transcend themselves to achieve a higher purpose which can only be done when they are living an Empowered Life. His goal is to shift the paradigm of the speaking industry by motivating, inspiring, and empowering people to impact the world. With his second book hitting the press, Alford is bound to take the world by storm to connect and coach the masses towards achieving their dreams and reaching their goals.

NEED AN EMPOWERING SPEAKER?

BOOK
ALFORD D. SIMON

FOR YOUR NEXT EVENT:

- Retreats
- Board Meetings
- Graduations
- Conferences
- Workshops
- Trainings
- Empowerment Sessions

- Seminars
- Symposiums
- Conventions
- Keynotes
- Coaching
- Consulation
- Forums & More!

CONTACT US

nfo@empowermentcoaching.org | www.empowermentcoaching.org

1-888-687-3380

Connect with Alford D. Simon on Social Media

Empowerment Coaching   @empowermentcoaching   @empower2impact

Made in the USA
San Bernardino, CA
18 June 2017